One Poet's Journey

A Picture Book of Poems

James Glassford

Copyright © 2024

All Rights Reserved

All rights reserved. No part of this book may be reproduced, distributed, or transmitted in any form or by any means, including photocopying, recording, or other electronic or mechanical methods, without the prior written permission of the publisher, except in the case of brief quotations embodied in critical reviews and certain other noncommercial uses permitted by copyright law.

This book is dedicated to my parents, who inspired me to appreciate poetry and the value of education at a young age.

Acknowledgment

I would like to acknowledge my wife Lynn for her photographs and her support and patience while I composed these poems. My friend Rob and my sister Sandra always encouraged me to write more. Cody and the Amazon team were also a great source of encouragement to me.

It would also like to acknowledge those who understand and appreciate the value and beauty of our natural world and work tirelessly to preserve and protect it for now and future generations.

Contents

Summer Sunrise 1

A Journey Through Time. 3

Life Friends 5

Beneath The Waves 7

Autumn's Song 9

Walking in a Winter Wonderland 11

Polar Bear 13

Wolverine 15

Nature And A Child's Mind 17

The Beaver 19

The Haida Totem Pole Carver 22

Memory Mat 24

Inner Peace 26

Ghostly Visions 28

Song of Solitude 30

Inner Troubles 32

Neptune's Ire 34

Songs of Spring 36

Scary Pirates 38

Seasons of Love 40

The Mountain Speaks 42

White Water Adventure 44

Muskoxen 47

Intertidal Pools 49

Mountain Stream 51

Garter Snake 54

The Tiger Swallowtail 56

Transcendental Man 59

The Buffalo and the Crow 62

Yaahl The Trickster 65

Dandelion 68

Alpine Meadow Magic 71

Summer Sunset 73

About the Author 75

Summer Sunrise

Sunrise in the mountains is a majestic and moving sight
It undresses the cloak of darkness and brings the world light
To the east a rosy blush begins as earth embraces the dawn
Curtains of night are lifted and its shadows soon withdrawn

Tendrils of light steal down the cavernous canyons tall
Like fingers of liquid lava running down a volcano wall
Caressing the cliffs and painting a sheen on their snowy faces
An artist's hand and a pastel palette touching many places

Tree by tree tree the forest takes on a new found tinge
The seas too are painted from their centre to their fringe
A kaleidoscope of colour as you watch the masterpiece unfold
With subtle grace and beauty like an alluring dream untold

Rays of sunlight kiss the soft belly of the fluffy clouds
Brushing them with chameleon colours endlessly endowed
The world awakens in the sun's tender soft-hued glow,
Each ray a promise, a new day of heartfelt hope to sow.

From darkness to light, there is a magical transition
A celestial ballet in a splendid and stately exhibition
The wind seems to whisper softly dispelling all fears
As a chorus of songbirds add their comforting cheers

The sun ascends faster now as purples turn to gold
Bringing its welcoming warmth and dispelling the cold
The sky is suddenly ablaze with the early morning light
Finally vanquishing the demons of the daunting night

Enjoy Nature's peace and grandeur as it percolates within
Let your heart be touched and feel a solemn serenity begin
Cast aside your worries, your troubles and your woes
As renewal begins and a blissful energy soon flows

A Journey Through Time.

In my youth, I saw the forest as a playground just for me
Where I could leap upon a log and perhaps a Tarzan be
The songs within my heart were there as I shouted at the hills
Bursting with the joy of living with all its fervour and thrills

Time seemed endless, then it had no meaning to this lad
One could wander these woodlands forever, never feeling sad
Days were filled with laughter with my soul and spirit free
Just me and my rainforest friends it was endless ecstasy

But youth is ever fleeting, and too soon, solemn duties called
The tasks were overwhelming me. I was anxious and appalled
There were deadlines and responsibilities, mortgages and debt
Sadness and sorrow and things one tries to forget

So I ventured to the trackless forest where I once played as a kid
And began seeing the woodlands now more clearly than I once did
The breezes blew gently on my frustrated and furrowed brow
The thrushes haunting songs, I remember even now

In the forest floor on a bed of moss, I leisurely lay
The verdant growth around me, where shadows softly play,
It carpets the ground here in a luscious display so fine
As Nature's quiet artist in the forest's emerald green design

Like a shaft of sun shining through a mournful morning mist
My clouds of despair lifted as if the earth itself was kissed
The siren song of Nature was an elixir to this troubled mind
As I unconsciously relived my youth and that long-lost happy time

So unburden your muddled mind, my friend, and set your spirit free
Let Nature help you look within, and soon you too will see
The strength to conquer all concerns and cast aside your cares
And all the many millstones that your saddled soul bares

Life Friends

Light played tag with shadows along the darkened wall
As the flickering fire reminded me of friendships, I recall
Some were just fire starters appearing early on in life
They started, flared and ended, a single note on a fife

Childhood friends going round and round on a painted horse
Circus clowns, Ferris wheels and cotton candy, of course
Teenage pals competing in Pokémon and video games
Camping trips sealed lips and special Codified names

Drive-in movies unwatched from the back seat of cramped cars
The screen but an excuse, petting and passions were the stars
Flickering flames of lost love affairs from the later years
Like blazes of lightning in a bottle that ended up in tears

Then came that certain someone so different from the rest
That somehow seems to be the one to end my romantic quest
They had that mysterious aura that was « je ne sais quoi »
Enchanting, intriguing, attractive and shining stars were all I saw

Throughout it all were old friends trustworthy, tried and true
Assisting me in tough times when I was too tired or blue
A helping hand, a gentle touch, a simple reassuring smile
A crutch when I needed it, they always went the extra mile

So make new friends but keep the old, as the ancient adage goes
Life may give you grief and sorrow and misfortunes in it's woes
But friends will laugh and cry with you and even share the blame
They make life worth living while enriching it all the same

Beneath The Waves

    The summer sun was slowly setting on the Salish Sea that day
Evocative and elegant seascapes that calmly take your breath away
Clouds were painted pastel pink with streaks of silver, red and gold
And the silence of this solitude was a particular pleasure to behold

An apparition appeared on the horizon, a ghostly spectre to be sure
Like a troubadour touting trouble it's dissonance was not demure
Shattering the stillness with a cacophony of commotion and noise
As raucous as a playground of squabbling children with their toys

Passengers were partying on a cruise ship, and they partied lots
Boisterous and belligerent bingers, they were brash and bellicose sots
They had marvelled at the mountains and gazed at glaciers grand
Scrambled up trails on side trips and seen the totems at Ketchikan

To them, it was all an adventure to be remembered with pride and praise
Unaware of what was happening hideously in the world beneath the waves
Churning propellers sliced through the sea, creating a scathing sound
That disturbed the many marine mammals for miles and miles around

Untreated sewage from bilge tanks was allowed to spew and pour
Distributing diseases and deadly viruses infecting shellfish and more
The caring custodians of the precious and once pristine shores there
Were now forsaken by a greedy government that didn't seem to care

The happy humpback whale that they watched and wondered at on Lanai
Was impaled on the bulbous bow of their ship, injured and left to die
Its death would go unnoticed by an unwary and thoughtless crew
They adored the almighty dollar and cared not what they plundered or slew

Those engines ran continuously, producing pollutants night and day
Without basic and elementary emission controls to help in any way
That's a million automobiles or more continually spewing soot
Degrading and damaging the delicate world setting troubles afoot

Awake from your slumber, oh sleeping world, for the reckoning hour is late
The ticking of the doomsday clock will too soon seal your fate
Clean up this malignant mess and correct your careless ways
Maybe, just maybe, a new dawn will see much better days

Autumn's Song

Storm clouds hug the horizon, mists encircle the summits like a wreath
Crimson colours paint the hilltops as frost festers on the leaves beneath
Soft summer breezes subdued now as the groaning gales of fall have begun
Glaring and gruelling summer heat replaced by a waning and watery sun

The sweet songs of summer are silent now, the autumn orchestras astir
There is a mellowness in the meadows where the warblers once were
Still, the magic muses of autumn sing their sylphic siren songs to me
Like Pan's flute in the fir forest or a mythical mermaid on the sea

I hear it in a gaggle of gabby geese, their formations flying so high
Like the trumpeting of trombonists as they pass swiftly by
The rustle of loose leaves as they scurry and scrape along the ground
Declaring to me their demise with a delicate and dolce sound

Bare branches like bony fingers scrape at my wide window pane
A brush whisking directly on a drum, on and then off again
Haunting howls of the autumn winds churn in long and lonely wails
Sounding like a troubled theremin that pierces and prevails

The pitter-patter of the rain once soft is now a sudden staccato roar
Heralding the cymbalic crash of Thor's trembling thunder once more
Crickets chirp constantly their mesmerizing hum as a final overture
Not as symphonic now as in summer, in fact somewhat demure

Moonlight shimmers stealthily as it plays tag with the cold clouds
It's dreamlike shadows concealing a screech owl within it's silky shrouds
He trills proud and poignantly like a piccolo or perhaps an alto flute
His sounds echoing erstwhile in the forest, solemn but resolute

Soon the wild winter winds will blow, and with it, a snowy silence bring
And the little brook that sang softly to me will sadly cease to sing
The cold earth will sleep so soundly beneath a silver snowy coat
That the anthems of the autumn will seem so distant and remote

Walking in a Winter Wonderland

The sun hugged the horizon, painting pastel patterns in the sky
Time for a winter walk in the forest, just my curious child and I
Another clear and crisp morning and another delightful day
With sunglasses, scarfs and snowsuits, we soon were on our way

His exuberance was infectious, there was anticipation in his eyes
What would the wilderness world bring, perhaps some big surprise
The outdoors is his classroom, and Nature provides the book
There is a tantalizing trove of treasures there, one only has to look

Silver crystals showered laces as our boots bit through the icy crust
Trekking along the trail today would be an adventure and a must
Gentle breezes blew softly, shaking snow off the fir trees all around
Glittering diamonds of pixie dust fluttered like feathers to the ground

A patch of perky popular trees, bare branches pointing at the sky
Looked like great giants waving their arms as if saying hello and hi
A flock of grey jays greeted us and landed lightly on my hand
Taking pieces of peanuts from me like Robin Hood and his merry band

Tiny tracks were scattered there. "Fairy footprints", my son exclaimed!
But they were from scampering squirrels and meadow mice, I explained
Mink and marten meandered here, even a moose to name but a few
These wild woodlands, on a winter day, were witness to a zestful zoo

A bevy of audacious otters had been sliding down the slippery slopes
Tobogganing in twos and tandem like some drunken and daring dopes
A silhouette was sitting silently, it's golden eyes glaring and aglow
It was a snowy owl scanning for motion in the barren bog below

Shadows slowly lengthened on this silvery scene we so admired
So this duo headed homeward, full of wonderment but very tired
The little lad soon fell asleep, a simple smile across his cherub cheeks
Dreaming of his adventures in the wild woodlands by the creeks

Polar Bear

To the Inuit people, he is Nanuq - mighty master, the biggest bear
A legendary and powerful predator, no other creature can compare
They see this beautiful bruin as resilient, resourceful and smart
In the basic balancing of Nature's book, he plays a peerless part

Shamans saw him as a spirit animal, a shapeshifter they knew
That transformed from white bear to man on entering an old igloo
This learned life form showed them how to hunt and harvest seal
To these northern natives, that was a needful and necessary deal

Meandering along, his muscles ripple like restless rapids in a stream
Exuding an air of self-confidence almost arrogant it would seem
His cream-coloured coat belies his presence in this cold arctic clime
Blending into the ice pack half-hidden, it is really quite sublime

A black roman nose and small eyes are the only visible clue
As he silently stalks his quarry to seize them and subdue
Today, the prize is a seal sleeping by a breathing hole in the ice
A sudden pounce and a swift blow or two will usually suffice

Other times, it's a wailing walrus pup or basking Beluga whales
They rarely escape his wily warriors ways, he usually prevails
Unchallenged and unforgiving this native ninja of the pole
Is not a senseless assassin, he is simply fulfilling his role

Now rising temperatures and thinning ice are threatening the north
The polar bears can't easily hunt seals or travel back and forth
Glaciers are retreating rapidly due to the harsh and harmful heat
Shrinking polar ice caps are signalling demise and imminent defeat

Polar bears are but a bellwether of deadly disasters yet to come
Sadly, this is a signal of how incredibly ignorant mankind has become
Why must these creatures carry this burden, much to our collective shame
Man has to heed the worrisome warnings now, for **he is** the one to blame

Wolverine

The northern lights were dancing a dazzling display in the starry sky
Greenish blue coloured curtains softly swaying as they passed by
The air was crisp and cold as icy winds whipped up the snow
Ignoring this, a wily wolverine was loping in the larches far below

This was not some Marvel mutant or a famous football team
Although he plays a real role in God's grand and glorious scheme
To the Innu, he was Carcajou, the clever creator of the earth
He possessed a special spirit and was a trickster full of mirth

His claws are curved like crampons, as if they were embossed
And his fur is hydrophobic, resistant to freezing and frost
Confident and courageous, he is wary, wild and untamed
A ferocious, fearless fighter once his testy temper is inflamed

He is seemingly small in stature, but what sets him so apart
Are claws and canines carved like steel and an iron heart
Wolf or bear or mountain lion it scarcely matters not
This formidable foe will fight them and will intimidate the lot

Gnarly and greedy, this glutton will scavenge any scrap of meat
Then spray it with his strong scent so opportunists cannot eat
A predator of other animals, whether massive or maybe small
With jaws and incisors that slash savagely-they have no chance at all

Alas, there is a battle brewing, an evil encounter he may not win
His domain is diminishing daily, and darker days are moving in
Sadly his species is threatened, man is driving their demise
And imminent extinction will soon be staring them in the eyes

Like many other sinless souls, these innocent icons of the free
Need vast and wild places to live in and set their spirits free
The mountains are their mecca the outdoors their domain
And conservation is the key if wilderness areas are to remain

Nature And A Child's Mind

One can generally guess or perhaps sometimes surmise
What the world looks like through a curious child's eyes
Only then could you possibly weave into a worthwhile phrase
The incipient images that a questioning mind might raise

A walk in the wild woods in the sunny summer times
Might remind that toddler of some old nursery rhymes
Their mind might even make up stories that magically match
The perfect pictures that only a vivid imagination can catch

A tall and towering tree that seems to split the sky
Might be Jack's beanstalk that quickly grew so high
While the thunder that rumbles and resonates up there
Could be the furious footsteps of the Ogre in his lair

The funny fat "fishy" swimming in the bubbling brook
Could be the one that Papa caught with his handy hook
A flat rock resting in the rubble was that a fat frying pan?
Like the one mama used to fry fish in for her little man.

Blueberries growing gorgeously in a bountiful bush nearby
Could they be the pretty plum plucked from Jack Horner's pie?
The ones that he extracted with his tiny thumb so spry
Exuberantly exclaiming out loud, "What a good boy am I"!

A shadow slipping by silently through the woods so shy
Was it the little baby bruin that Goldilocks did spy
Or Winnie the Pooh Bear, who so liked his healthy honey
That he got stuck in the doorway of his friend the bunny?

Joyful journey over, its time to happily head on back
With that child prattling proudly about adventures along the track
Fresh experiences savoured and a few fairy tales coming to life
Far from the noise of the city with its polluted air and strife

You too can only imagine what goes through any child's mind
In the world of wonders that awaits them in the natural world to find
So take your inquisitive child along to wonder and endlessly explore
On a walk in the wilderness that awaits you just outside your door

The Beaver

The summer sun was setting on a peaceful, placid pond
It's fading light disappearing in the forests just beyond
The dying rays were captured in the ripples of a wake
Shimmering and moving, chasing shadows down the lake

Something was swimming silently in the tepid twilight there
Moving slowly and cautiously with confidence and care
Too massive for a muskrat, it was too minuscule for a moose
Not a dropping of diving ducks or even some silly goose

To the natives, he was known as Amik, the custodian of the land
They revered and worshipped him, and they seemed to understand
A tireless and talented worker and an energetic engineer
Hydrologist and forester, a dedicated dam builder without peer

Trees are carved and chiselled by his awesome orange teeth
He then fells and fashions them to drag across the heath
With webbed feet and a wide fat tail, steadfast about his work
Carefully crafting a barrier and trapping water in a cirque

That levee restricts the river flows and regulates the streams
Filtering the waters and creating helpful habitats, it seems
Now a refreshing reservoir, residual water in times of drought
That all the forest denizens simply cannot survive without

Dams create deep pools and winter worlds for all the fishes
Wetlands for the moose and elk and vegetation for their dishes
Dams open special spaces and let the soft sunlight in
Warming the shallow waters where the circles of life begin

Amik works with the waters and the waters bring forth life
Plants and animals together without rancour, without strife
Setting a fine example of managing the wilderness and wild
Sharing his blessed bounty, unlike a petulant and pouty child

Yes, we are indebted to this beaver, a symbolic icon of our land
He creates an enduring environment that is so carefully planned
Reflecting on the destruction that modern man has wrought
We must learn the lessons that busy beaver has tacitly taught

So emulate Amik's work to repair and restore the wild
Clean up the mess that man has left degraded and defiled
The task that lies before you is so obvious and glaring
Courage then to do it awaits the dauntless and the daring

The Haida Totem Pole Carver

A well-weathered totem pole stands, still guarding the sacred land
Carefully carved from a cedar tree by a Haida craftsman's hand
It was once part of the woodlands with no discerning shape or form
A great giant flourishing in the forest as was the island's norm

A curious carver saw it there and envisioned so much more
His ancestral souls spoke to him, and now he knew his chore
Somehow, he must unshackle the spirits seemingly trapped within
Deciding to delicately free them, he knew his work must soon begin

With chisels, an adze, a carving knife, plus various other tools
He set about the tedious task, following sacred and ancient rules
The totem, a special symbol, a revered representative of his clan
A hallmark of his heritage, standing for every woman, child and man

The scent of cedar filled the air, and wood chips fell like rain
His back and arms ached endlessly, but he could feel no pain
Sweat soaked his stained shirt and stung his tired eyes
But the vision in his mind was firmly focused on the prize

An elegant eagle standing proud, sculpted with wings spread and spry
Was positioned precisely atop the pole, the royal ruler of the sky
Resting beneath him, a raucous raven, a tease and trickster to the core
The legendary, loquacious one that lingers large in native lore

Wolf, known as the patient pathfinder was carved into the wood
He was a hero hunter, loyal and loving, that was always good
Finally there was an ornate Orca, the sovereign of the seas
Who guided missing mariners and put their minds at ease

Finished long ago, the totem's fancy facade faded to ghostly grey
Chiseled by the winds of fate, it's weathered faces worn away
Its haunting beauty and spirit though, still watch over Haida Gwaii
Reminding me of the traditions and values here as I patiently paddle by

The old craftsman carver too, is sadly mourned in old Massett town
His skills a memory in the mists of time, his craft passed on down
Students studied this artist and many mastered the ancient art
Traditions and carvings were cherished, he had played his part

Memory Mat

There's a well-worn welcome mat outside my kitchen door
Half-faded fibres filled with "yarns' and oh so much more
Its grey gingham is gathered, and so intricately interweaved
In a pretty pattern that a careful knitter cleverly conceived

On its surface haphazardly hangs a handful of matted hair
From my canine companions that often calmly curled up there
Outdoor adventures and walks were their calling and their creed
Fortunately, time spent with me fondly fulfilled a natural need

One Poet's Journey

A pink petal there, perhaps from a pleasant peace rose flower
The one that blooms so beautifully beside the garden bower
I often sat there in sacred silence to muse and meditate
Alone with Mother Nature in a calm and tranquil state

Grains of granite granules from a majestic mountain-high
Where I gazed on in wonderment at the grandeur beneath my eye
And I breathed in the scent of Daphne in the cold, clear alpine air
Enraptured by the sylvan scenes that lay before me there

Particles of paint peeled off a favourite fishing lure
Memories of magic moments that meaningfully endure
Quiet and peaceful paddles on pretty and placid lakes
Wilderness and wildlife there in the images my mind makes

Fine fir needles scattered by a billowy and boisterous breeze
Remind me of the many meanderings that put my mind at ease
A simple stroll or saunter along footpaths in the fertile forest edge
Or a mosey through the nearby marsh with its bullrushes and sedge

Unseen tears of sorrow and sadness, the stains are there for all to see
Recalling friends and lovers lost that once meant so much to me
Drifting in and out like mists - childhood friends and others in later life
Sharing joy and happiness or enduring mutual pain and strife

These are but some memories in my proverbial magic mat
Each of us has one, and it's remarkably unique at that
So cherish each moment and store them in your mirthful mind
Reliving and recollecting is such a soothing balm you'll find

Inner Peace

A silent soul seated in a seemingly sedate repose
Like a single sitting Buddha, one surely might suppose
This refuge for reflection was a placid place of peace
Where beauty and tranquillity were its only altarpiece

He had left behind a world of pain, trouble and doubt
Of conflagration, corruption, famine and drought
Murder and mayhem in the cheerless city streets
Avarice and anger, callous criminals and cheats

In quiet solitude here, he sought an elusive inner calm
Knowing mindful meditation was both a blessing and a balm
Light played with shadows in the steep canyons of his mind
Revealing inner strengths there he thought he'd left behind

Inwardly, his thoughts played on in plain picture words
Scenes of serenity that only a mellow mind conjures
Imagining an archangel tending to a child with grace
That angel seemed to wear his long-lost mother's face

Childhood friends going round and round on a painted horse
Circus clowns, Ferris wheels and cotton candy, of course
Teenage pals competing in Pokémon and video games
Camping trips sealed lips and special Codified names

Drive-in movies unwatched from the back seat of cars
The screen but an excuse, petting and passion were the stars
Flickering flames of puppy love from the younger years
Laughter in a school lunchroom, tenderness and tears

Evoking memories of childhood and his naive innocence
Blotted out his biggest burdens in a very real sense
Needing no narcotics or a liquid fix to ease his woes
He threw off his troubles and cast aside his withering woes

Refreshed now and relaxed from his transcendental time
He had cast aside cares and doubts in a manner most sublime
Meditation brings solace putting stress and strife in its place
Pause patiently and look within, and serenity you'll embrace

Ghostly Visions

A thick fog enveloped the seaside and really so much more
Cloaking all with an eerie silence and shrouding the shore
Undaunted, I cavalierly launched my canoe on a rocky beach
Near a placid but practical point at a river's rugged reach

I paddled fecklessly into the face of the forbidding unknown
It was very tense as it seemed I was entering the twilight zone
Bewildered and befuddled I squinted but could scarcely see
Soon, wreathlike the foggy curtain in a wicked wall encircled me

There was nothing visible ahead and nothing visible behind
No landmarks or reference points, I might as well be blind
I sensed my soul's loud pleading - danger was very near
My heart then skipped a beat, I was frozen and filled with fear

Nearby, something made a wake and then a sudden splash
My great worries weren't unfounded, faint hope was swiftly dashed
Something large was lingering near, I sensed doom and dread
Davey Jones's Locker was calling, could it be my deathbed?

A black triangular shape knifing carefully through the mire
Would my fearful life soon be over, was I about to expire?
A great white shark, perhaps on its habitual hungry quest?
My teeth chattered nervously - I was truly stressed

Alas all the demons surfaced and breached quite near my boat
A pod of killer whales, a trace of tightness lingered in my throat
They were honed in and hunting yes, but I was not their prey
This foolish adventurer would paddle on and live another day

The sun soon shattered the mists like a pin bursting a balloon
With confidence, it restored my bravery once so badly strewn
This naive nitwit then navigated the canoe back to the rocky strand
Grateful once more and thankful to be on solid, sensible land

Song of Solitude

There's a secret place where the restless oceans flow
That my fellow man seems not to understand or know
It's a refuge from society's strifes and its vexing storms
Where Mother Nature sets the mood with it's noble norms

It's a quiet cove, a sanctuary on the scenic Salish sea
There I muse and meditate - it sets my soaring spirits free
The changing tides and rhythms of the lonely lapping waves
Are a miracle of melody with many musical octaves

The seagulls cry with joy and the ebullient eagles screech
As they ride the breezes effortlessly above this lonely beach
At sea a pod of Orcas hunt, while playful dolphins dance
Humpback whales spout and breech in this vast expanse

Gentle ocean breezes blow and caress my carefree cheeks
While I admire the allure and beauty of distant snow capped peaks
Suddenly a twig snaps revealing two fawns and a doting doe
Close by a watchful wood thrush sings its song so soft and low

A large white erratic boulder defies the challenges of the sea
It's a rock of untold ages that remains resolute for all to see
Weathered logs line the shore lying loose in a haphazard way
Like many matchsticks cast aside by a boisterous boy at play

There is no finer place I know to rest and harmonize my soul
To calm and rejuvenate one's mind and make one's heart whole
This is the solace of solitude, a secret society for a favoured few
Mother Natures pacifying place, my memories and my id too

Take a moment and wander to your special place nearby
Just you and Mother Nature the wilderness and the sky
Breathe in the bounteous beauty let it seep into your very core
And an inner peace you'll find there for now and evermore

Inner Troubles

Like a song you keep hearing repeatedly in your head
It played upon my psyche and filled my mind with dread
Pervasive thoughts and emotions were meddling with my day
Useful and rational thinking, it seems, had gone another way

Calling upon my inner self to chase those intangibles away
I sauntered slowly on a path beside a quiet ocean bay
Lazy clouds floated overhead as I sat and stopped to stare
Wondering why others understood, but no one deigned to care

A solitary thrush sang there, and a babbling brook entwined
Their ethereal ensemble was more than music to my mind
Then the wind whispered wistfully and gently combed my hair
Raindrops seemed to wash away the stresses in the air

The floral scent of honeysuckle was an exquisite elixir too
As a bracing sea breeze cleared my muddled mind anew
Unburdened now of emotions that painted such a sorry scene
Wilderness brushed aside my thoughts and wiped my canvas clean

The storms in my mind I realized had raged for much too long
Nature had purged my problems now and gave my spirits song
By calmly contemplating the world in a mindful meditative state
In the undisturbed calmness there I had set my spirits straight

Once beset with thoughts that endlessly seemed to brood
I had summoned the strength within to cast off my melancholic mood
Homeward I turned now, knowing that Nature had done its part
The joy of life lingered on and dwelt within my happy heart

Neptune's Ire

Broken promises, broken dreams, fecklessness, or so it seems
The placid seashore sadly screams as on its surface oil gleams
Waves that once lapped leisurely on rough rocks and silver strands
Now, carry poisonous refuse from many callous and careless hands

Garbage, garbage everywhere diverse and damaged plastic things
Cartons, containers and ghost nets even discarded cello strings
In the great pacific garbage patch, three times the size of France
Covering the Pacific ocean, where delightful dolphins used to dance

Nature is sadly suffering caught in a disastrous deathly spire
The bounteous beauty we once knew will soon sadly expire
Polar ice is melting as great mountain glaciers dwindle away
The air and waters are swiftly warming each and every day

Soon, Neptune will rise in his watery kingdom with anger and pain
Witnessing the wanton destruction seething with dread and disdain
He will call out Tempestas and perhaps Jupiter and Vulcan too
To deal with this disastrous dilemma and do what they must do

You have finally done it, mankind - you've rang the doomsday bell
By ignoring the environment now, you will clearly hear it's knell
Sharon's boat awaits you, and Cerberus is there as well
To carry you over the river Styx through the gnarly gates of hell

The time has come, the Soothsayers say to amend your ways
The future is bleak already we do not have too many days
So repent all you silly sinners, repent before it's too late
Or the fists of fate will find you and finally seal your fate

Songs of Spring

Sometime in a melancholy March, you sense change is in the air
Winter is losing its icy grip, and spring has left its latent lair
Perhaps it is the waft of welcome warmth that falls upon a cool cheek
Or the brisk bubbling of the babbling brook, perchance the chilly creek

There is no magic moment, no solitary or nearest number
That announces Nature's awakening from its winter slumber
And yet you feel a restlessness and struggle to somehow cope
As you look longingly for the first flowers, the messengers of hope

Perhaps it's a snowdrop poking through the shrivelling snow
A witch hazel, forsythia or creeping phlox, you never really know
That something stirs emotions and puts a spring in every stride
Clears the cold cobwebs of winter and leaves you misty-eyed

An ode to joy now fills the air the siren songs of spring are there
The burdened earth is free at last to shed its weary winter wear
Forests that once were wrapped in the silence of snow so deep
Now, awaken to the sounds of hatchlings and their constant peep

The rallying cry of snow-white swans on high slowly drifting down
While in the woods and waters, there is a musical melody all around
You begin to feel it in your bones, you hear it with your ears
The rebirth and resurrection of the earth as it has been for countless years

The chilly curtain has been lifted now and a pristine play begins anew
It's an old familiar script you love with the actors you already knew
But each passing year as it begins again you embrace its Sylphic song
With rejuvenated hope and joy, you wholeheartedly sing along

So always remember the songs of spring and keep them in your heart
For those days of sorrow or sadness when your world needs a fresh start
They will brighten the daunting darkness and the dread of a dismal day
Cast out the demons of despair and discreetly help you on your way

Scary Pirates

I sauntered slowly into a seaside second-hand store
Searching for any naval antiques which I admire and adore
Commanding one corner - a mammoth, menacing man
Was he the building block of Blackbeards bellicose clan?

He stood six foot seven or so and surely seventeen stone
A mass of meaty muscle, not simply skin and bone
An eye patch, a bandana and, for his hand, a hook
A flintlock in his pantaloons to discourage any crook

With a loose leather jerkin and by the cut of his jib
You wouldn't dare mess with him or even try to fib
"Ahoy there landlubber," he said with a curt scowl
In a deep-throated tone, sounding more like a growl

I hurried down the aisle as my hands began to shake
Afraid of the aftermath should anything fall or damn it break!
Spotting a silver spyglass shining in the limited light
I held it to my wondering eye, it gave me such a fright

The glass was a little hazy, like fog or mist upon the sea
But when it cleared, a bustling brigantine was there for me to see
Its Jolly Roger flew proudly above the mainsail on the mast
While buccaneers belted out "merchant ship, ahoy and avast"

Its cannons boomed out their cacophony, belching fire and smoke
An acrid odour ensued then, as I sputtered and I choked
Barbed boarding hooks bit in like harpoons in a whale
Pirates stormed the stricken ship like leaves before a gale

"Stop you scurvy scoundrels or you'll simply be shark bait
There's gold beneath your gunnels we want it and will not wait
We will give no quarter lads, so furl up your silver sails
Or our cutlasses will carve you up cos dead men tell no tales"

Appalled, I placed the glass back into its larcenous leather case
Afraid of witnessing mass murders - that I simply could not face
Startled, scared and shaken, I stealthily slipped out of the store
This snapshot of history rattled me, I could take no more

Seasons of Love

She was like a simple snow drop flower emerging from the ground
He was like a single spring peeper belting out his joyful sound
They somehow found each other near a peaceful, placid place
Two single souls came together in a fond and friendly embrace

Like maple sap rising beneath the firm and furrowed bark
Their passion seemed to pursue a robust rainbow arc
Together, they were better than any two souls set apart
A union of seductive senses, a harmony of the heart

As spring became summer, emotions were endlessly entwined
Like roses on a garden arbour or passion flowers on a vine
Breezes were warm and gentle, there was laughter in the rain
They knew this was a romance that they could never find again

They dreamily drifted on in cupid's sea of endless charm
Swilling the sweet wine of love and cuddling arm-in-arm
In a cool canopy of shade, words were whispered and promises made
As in their robes of youth and fire, their symphony they played

Too soon the sun's warmth began to fizzle and fade so fast
As the sonata songs of summer came to a sad end at last
Soprano notes they had cherished then changed to a profundo bass
As the mistress of melancholy slowly entered their embrace

They had sipped from the coveted chalice, the ambrosia of love
But it was slipping from their careless fingers like a ghostly glove
Aphrodite had abandoned them and Eros was departing too
They were retreating from each others arms, what was there to do?

The woeful winds of winter ushered in more uncertainty and unease
Concerns crept in like storm clouds on a sudden shifting breeze
Tears replaced the laughter and sadness usurped the bliss
Love's symphony had ended without a parting kiss

The Mountain Speaks

I was born in searing smoke, ferocious fire and seismic quakes
A traumatic birth, a beginning where liquid lava cools and bakes
I revealed myself like the Phoenix in a flaming fountain of fire
Where the Vulcan Gods and Pele release their fury and their ire

Over eons and ages, I gradually cooled and greatly grew
A child of the early earth and its tectonic and toxic brew
Stately now a tranquil obelisk towering tall and high
My spires serenely splitting the saintly sanctity of the sky

Ice Ages once crowned me with my stately silver cap
Snowfalls added to it and now I wear this regal wrap
I faithfully fed wild waters that tumbled down my steep slope
It filled the streams and rivers and brought the world hope

The wicked winds of change are blowing now and they only blow ill
The temperature are rising, but my glaciers need the cold and chill
Snow and ice need freezing frosts like rivers need refreshing rain
Sadly climate changes are shouting a warming and worrisome refrain

Far up in the airy alpine where my summits kiss the azure sky
The goats still cling close to craggy cliffs and eagles effortlessly fly
But a trickle of tears now tumble from the soft and shrivelling snow
And begin their jarring journey to the verdant valleys down below

My glaciers seem to be crying, their time coming to a sorrowful end
Forsaken and forgotten, they slowly bleed but cannot mend
Like a receding hairline on a famously full and handsome head
Fast fading into oblivion and hanging by a thin and tenuous thread

Rivers and streams that raged once are receding and running slow
Crops, fish and wildlife are perishing from a persistent lack of flow
The powerful polar caps are dwindling and melting into the sea
While wicked tides are restlessly rising, encircling you and me

Mankind must surely listen, but alas, he will not hear
The drumbeat of his avarice drowns out his world so dear
He is destined to a cruel end and such will be his fickle fate
Unless he acts boldly and quickly before it is too late

White Water Adventure

Its wild, white waters are calling, and I can't really resist
Another enjoyable encounter like a lively lovers tryst
A sensation of solitude along the scenic sylvan shore
The lyrics of a lonely loon who could ask for more?

The paddle singing peacefully with every single stroke
Was more than a musical melody to this blithe bloke
Chattering, babbling brooks joined in - a soothing sound
Just the joy of Nature on the lake to comfort all around

I slip into the river now and sense a sudden change
Flecks of foam along the shore where ragged rocks range
The pianissimo sounds are past, now I hear a definitive drum
It's hurried heartbeat sounding like a sinister sitar strum

Wicked walls are rising and worrisome waters are running fast
Orchestrating chaos in their cantankerous crescendo blast
In the deep darkness dead ahead, I hear the threatening knell
Is that the cacophony of Cerebus calling me to hell?

Speeding swiftly now around big, barbaric bends
Roaring like a lion trapped, the river dangerously descends
Rugged rocks - a minefield beneath this beastly brew a boiling
Awaiting my errant arrival, like a venomous viper coldly coiling

With my pulse racing rapidly and a tightness in my chest
I plunge into the terrible task at hand and try my very best
Front stroke, back stroke, now left, no veer to the right!
Fighting cruel current with all my stamina and might

My tired arms are aching and yet I feel no pain
My torso is twisted but there is no sense of strain
I cautiously follow the currents, careful lest I capsize
Or a watery grave might mark my disastrous demise

Then suddenly, it's over just as quickly as it began
Am I the conquering hero, a masterful and mighty man?
Perhaps I'm just a Prima Donna who has to prove his mettle
Who sees the raging river ride as yet another score to settle

This adrenaline rush unleashes a drive to fulfill man's primal needs
To satisfy his senses and engage in dangerous and daring deeds
Why else would men climb mountains - just because they're there?
Or free fall fast and foolishly through footless halls of air?

Muskoxen

He's the titan of the tundra - a peerless polar prince
Emerging many millennia ago, he has been there ever since
Braving bitter cold, he leads his bold and beloved band
The head of a hearty herd in this bleak and barren land

To the Inuktituk, he is Umingmak or the bearded one
An icon of a culture centred in the land of the midnight sun
He provides them with provisions that fulfill many roles
Like meat and milk to feed them and wool to warm their souls

Whipped by wild winds, he wears a weighty woollen coat
That quiviut is more precious than skeins from any cashmere goat
He has short legs and is stocky with a shaggy shoulder hump
On a barrel-shaped body, you might even call him plump

His harem was huddled hungrily on the highest hill
Swilling wild willows their waiting hunger to fullfil
The big bull stopped suddenly, there was trouble in the air
Sensing smoke and fire, burning bushes were everywhere

The hysterical herd panicked and parted in a raucous rush
Cows and calves together skirting any bovid crush
Off the high hill, they hurried to swim across a shielding stream
Safe and sound for the moment or so it would somehow seem

But things are unsettled, there is unease in the universe
Temperatures are rising and quickly getting worse
Permafrost is thawing, releasing captured carbon in the air
The ice caps are melting, it's more than Mother Earth can bear

Mega-mines and oil pipelines plunder this pristine land
While pitiful politicians don't seem to care or understand
They'll steal the Arctic refuge for some dollars and a "friend"
Regardless of the result for the muskoxen or any denizen

So wake up, you woeful world, the time to change is getting late
Climate change is coming fast it could soon seal our feckless fate
The muskoxen miseries are many, but that is just the sad and single start
It's the canary in a coal mine that will tragically tear us all apart

Intertidal Pools

Two curious children rested on a rock by the Salish sea
Looking now at the many life forms they could clearly see
Stretching in front of them a peaceful inter-tidal pool
More miracles on display here than in any single school

A microcosm lay before them there, a marvelous, mini-world
So much to see and scrutinize as this spectacle unfurled
There were barnacles and limpets, seaweeds and snails
Sculpins and Blennys and fantastic fish with funny tails

Little critters whose first name so often starts with "sea"
Like stars, slugs and urchins, even some anemone
Prawns, periwinkles and whelks, to name just a few
Even a baby octopus you seldom see in any zoo

There was a mudskipper moving madly there
He could maneuver in the mud and breathe the salty air
The children watched in wonder at this famous fish
Until he dove into his burrow with a sudden swish

In the distance, they dimly saw a humpback whale breach
And dancing dolphins dawdling not too far from the beach
A family of otters frolicked furiously in the crashing surf
High overhead, an eagle slowly scanned his sacred turf

The tide then turned again with its rapid and relentless rise
Time to turn homeward now, enlightenment in their eyes
Lessons learned at the seaside they would not soon forget
Magic moments to cherish and keep in memories net

Tide pools are pockets of sea abandoned by the tide
A perfect place for learning, where many creatures hide
A cornucopia of characters dancing in a salty sea of calm
It soothes the saddened spirit more than any aromatic balm

This is truly a treasure chest we simply cannot ignore
We must all pull together to preserve our pristine shore
Plastic particles and pollution are taking a terrible toll
The ocean is a wild and wondrous place, not our toilet bowl

Mountain Stream

When the woeful world seems dark and dreary
And I trudge along with a heavy heart so weary
There's a special sanctuary where I sit and rest
Peace and solitude there, at its blissful best

It's just a meandering moving mountain stream
That seems to somehow start a dewy-eyed dream
I sit on a smooth stone that is stationed there
And let the soothing sounds take me somewhere

The whispering waters seem to talk to me
As in a mirthful pianissimo soliloquy
It softly sings a song in its buoyant babble
As its cold water washes the toes that I dabble

My mind melds with the mountain stream and sky
I reflect on my youth and yesteryears gone by
In places where the falling fountains ripple
I'd skipped stones and hoped to make a triple

The fleeting shadows in the shallow streams
Were like schools of stealthy submarines
A dragonfly that dashed and darted to and fro
Was a helicopter hauling horses don't you know?

A funny face in the mirrored water I suddenly see
Could that funny face really be a monster or me?
Or is it just a crazy and cagey, clever clown
Inviting me to plunge in, perhaps to drown?

The staccato sound of a partridge drumming
Was the percussion piece to the streams humming
The flute-like trill of the wary wood thrush
Echoed through the dense woodland brush

The delicate aroma of the earth and pine
Remind me of those youthful days of mine
The sweet smell of a woodland honeysuckle
Brings up many memories and I softly chuckle

Moments and memories that I remember and cherish
A refuge from a world so superficial and garish
As I ramble home, now refreshed and renewed
My spirits soaring and sad thoughts eschewed

So when your own world seems a trifle troubled
And your worries mount as if they'd doubled
Noble Nature calmly awaits any commune or call
She's a top-drawer therapist - the best of all

Garter Snake

He weaved his way warily through the wild flowers and bees
Like a wrapping ribbon wriggling in the bosom of a breeze
He was cool but calm in the fresh, clean mountain air
Lethargic and mere meters from his lonely latent lair

A big round rock for basking in the mid-morning sun
Would refresh and reenergize him until he was done
Then, he would slowly slip off it and be on his way
A serpent searching silently for any unwary prey

With his double-tipped tongue lashing like a wild whip
He slowly began his lethargic and lackadaisical trip
A tiny trace of tell-tale odour from some prized prey
Would send a signal and he would slowly slither that way

A little leopard frog leaped just beyond his unhinged jaw
An errant escapee from a mean and malicious maw
One haughty hawk hunting from the heavens on high
Almost snatched the snake - saved by a bunny nearby!

A meandering mouse floundered and became a fateful feed
He savoured and swallowed it slowly fulfilling his natural need
Lethargic now and listless with a difficult duty he would dread
His small skin scales spoke to him - it was time to shed

Lidless eyes that could only stare turned almost milky blue
As shedding lots of now slack skin would certainly ensue
Some ancient seers saw this as a sign of immortality
Serpent worship was seen as sacred in their spirituality

In the bible, Satan is seen as a serpent in the Garden of God
Enticing Adam and Eve and thus banishing them abroad
No snake would have to hear this they really have no ears
They are shy and simple souls despite our unfounded fears

So if you should stumble on this snake, at the very least
Fear not his fangs or fury he is not a savage beast
He is not there to harm you he is part of Nature's schemes
Like the forest and the fields, the lakes and the streams

The Tiger Swallowtail

Here's a Cinderella story, a somewhat tragic tale
About a beautiful butterfly called a Tiger Swallowtail
Its wide wings are burnished in black and golden hues
This *Papilio canadensis* has bits of blue and orange too

Shimmering in the summer sun and soaring in the light
A dazzling display of dancing - quite a stunning sight
That's not a detailed depiction, only a virtual vignette
Fluttering in a field of flowers is a scene you can't forget

This featherless flyer was once small and green and round
A trivial thing tethered to a leaf and loosely bound
That egg became a green caterpillar with a stocky, snake-like head
Yellow dots and illusory eyes that predators would dread

Munching its way through tender leaves, whether sweet or sour
It's greed and gluttony growing with each and every hour
Then suddenly a subtle change, as a stirring starts within
Forming a shell around itself as transformations begin

A chrysalis becomes a humble home in which to hibernate
A shelter from the winter storms, a pithy pause to pupate
Soon springtime sun sends welcome warmth and now a change
Something happens within and that something is strange

What was once a creepy creature worm-like or so it appeared
Was now this beautiful butterfly respected and revered
Like Cinderella at the ball and the infamous glass slipper
The caterpillar cast off it's clothes as if unzipping a zipper

It widened its wings and sailed away as summer breezes blew
Waltzing in the warm wind as it wished and wanted to
Jiving on a puff of air and playing peacefully by the hour
It seemed to sample sweet nectar from each and every flower

But existence is an ephemeral thing, the fateful hour had come
It's earthly time had ended, and this acrobatic angel did succumb
I knew its life had ended when I saw its torn and tattered wings
Still I was glad and grateful for the joy that a butterfly brings

Sometimes in life's journey as moments and memories, we reap
We deem someone as dubious by the appearances they keep
Remember the story of the chrysalis, and you may then discover
That you cannot simply judge a book by the picture on it's cover

Transcendental Man

He was a man of means by any measure of success
The extent of his expansive empire was anybody's guess
But all this fame and fortune took a harsh and heavy toll
It robbed him of his happiness and emptied out his soul

Everyday conspired to cloak any chance of inner peace
The real road to recovery meant this lifestyle must surely cease
So he empty his own agenda and cleared the clutter and the strife
And opening his heavy heart, he searched for a simple ascetic life

Now he sat musing like a monastic monk in a monastery
Cloistered in a log cabin now, a new life its beneficiary
Flickering lantern light danced on a transcendental, tranquil scene
And the solitude embraced him as if in a satiating dream

The Northern lights were dancing - coloured curtains in the sky
They reflected off the frozen lake and the verdant forest nearby
There was no one here to speak to in this wilderness apart
He could feel and hear the music in the eardrum of his heart

When he moved his canoe leisurely along the lengthy lakes
To the haunting call of a lonely loon and the splash a paddle makes
The silence of this solitude stirred a certain certitude within
And shaped his perceptions and made his spirits grin

A taste of wild strawberries or the starry skies at night
A bull moose splashing in the shallows, otters playing in delight
These were but one portrait of the many pictures playing in his mind
As the creature's spirits in this wilderness world helped him to unwind

He lived a life of grace and gratitude just for the sake of being
For all that Mother Nature taught him and all that he was seeing
He had found boundless freedom in the bosom of his God
And shed the shackles that bound him, and he was truly awed

He could not stay forever in this precious and pristine place
Where one could contemplate life at a slow and steady pace
Nature's solitude had healed him as only Nature can
And he turned home again a more introspective man

We all should take a minute, sixty seconds to contemplate
Is our current life fulfilling? What is missing on our plate?
There is a world of Nature waiting just beyond your door
Embrace the silent solitude, and you will find so much more

The Buffalo and the Crow

A belligerent brown bison bantered with a cunning crow
As he bellowed out his woes to the deep and drifting snow
My ancient ancestors were monarchs and ruled this lovely land
Every patch of pristine prairie was held by their command

They were rumored to be a mass of more than sixty million strong
They grazed and gathered here - a testy and truculent throng
Their hooves sounded like thunder and raised towering torrents of dust
That blocked the shining sun and turned its yellow hues to rust

The native nations revered them, the Cheyenne, Blackfoot and Sioux
Arapaho, Apache and Assiniboine, to name a few
Following massive bison migrations, they lived a nomadic life
An interwoven existence like a leather scabbard and its knife

The bison provided food, pelts and even string for beads
All the basic necessities that a close community needs
The natives only took the infirm, the injured, weak and frail
One's that wouldn't make it, the ones most easy to avail

The winds of change were blowing and from a distant land
Came early explorers who couldn't care or understand
Finding new frontiers or lands was their destiny and desire
Uncovering pristine riches for their powerful patrons to acquire

Then, like hordes of hungry locusts, countless scores of settlers came
Spanish, French and English - things would never be the same
Trains of covered wagons, teams of oxen and all their chattel
Long guns and skilful soldiers well prepared for any battle

They destroyed the fertile plains and the native grasslands too
Tattered tracks from wagon wheels as their numbers grew and grew
They slaughtered the herds of bison and destroyed the Indian nations
Exterminated the bewildered beasts and exiled the natives to reservations

Buffalo Bill Cody and his gratuitous, gun-toting crew
We're admired as heroes for all the buffalo they slew
These men had no understanding, never tried to appreciate
The terrible toll they had taken, until it was too late

The cunning crow was silent as to his sudden surprise
The great bull bison trembled, there were tears in his eyes
Many years had passed yet he still sensed with deep regret
The deep loss his ancestors felt in memories even yet

Yellowstone is now a place American Bison can call home
Where they freely breed and congregate and can readily roam
This sorrowful saga is a testament to the greed of the common man
As sadly, other critters perish with no such considerations or plan

Yaahl The Trickster

The trickster Raven, replete with his supernatural sway
Stared down at the world from his perch so very far away
All the creatures there had a spirit and that spirit was as one
It moved meaningfully between them under a solitary sun

He had stolen the sun for them, made the moon and the stars
Filled the heavens with planets like Venus, Jupiter and Mars
Creating inland lakes, rippled rivers and sweet streams
Tranquil trees and friendly forests in a land of many dreams

He divided day and night and set them together in motion
And also ruled the rhythm of the tides in the vast ocean
Placing fish in the waters and animals in this sylvan land
Even giving man fire as he had so precisely planned

Then Raven vanished and took away his sacred spirit power
Creatures couldn't communicate, things got glum and very dour
Men could talk to each other but animals couldn't understand
A silent sadness spread over a now tense and troubled land

Still man can convey his feelings with his empathy and his eyes
Or with a gentle gesture or deed should the need arise
We may no longer have with animals this sacred spirit to share
But can readily reveal to them that we are the ones that care

Some men understood this and were careful custodians of the land
Cultivating Nature's ways and working with it hand in hand
Then the God of greed took over and the lure of lucre prevailed
The vision of the dream disappeared and sadly wisdom failed

The fish that once flourished were destroyed and decimated by greed
The forests were ravished relentlessly beyond any natural need
Factories spewed out their poisons into the foul and fetid air
The sultry planet sizzled endlessly as it suffered everywhere

Now the path that lies before us we must rapidly rearrange
Or face a world of uncertainly and even more unwelcome change
The ice caps are steadily melting, and the oceans soon will quickly rise
The price of postponement is, for us all, a dark and deadly demise

So stop raping the old forests let them flourish and revive
Quit contaminating our lakes and streams, help keep them all alive
Eliminate the endless emissions that pollute the air like CO_2
Everyone must do their part, and that even means you too!

Dandelion

I meandered through some meadows one early May morn
In the brisk and breezy mountain air, I felt almost reborn
As I crested a rocky ridge, a sudden sight to behold
A field of fabulous flowers, a field filled with gold

Its denizens were dandelions that dazzled in the sun so much
While waving in the wind, it seemed they had the Midas touch
The mature ones had puffy heads like perfect parachutes
That float freely on a breath of air before they put down roots

As I rested there in that serene sea of glittering golden yellow
My restive spirit softened became more mild, meek and mellow
The dapper drift of dandelions seem to softly speak to me
In a very verdant voice you could not hear or even see

In France, I am deemed "dent de Lion", or the lion's tooth
Honestly, I have a many names if I'm to tell the truth
The Québécois say Pissenlit (that's how I'm addressed)
Since "enlit" means "in bed" in French (you can guess the rest)

Those English chaps prefer to call me Blowball instead
As children like to blow the seeds off my puffy head
I am designated Dumble-Dor by the nascent Newfie crowd
And you can call me anything, but call me patently proud

I provide nutritious nectar that the busy bumblebees savour
My achenes are a seed source that the blissful birds favour
My leaves are a nutritious source of vitamins like A, K and C
There is also iron, copper and potassium you see

Some say I'm just a troubling and terrible, tenacious pest
Others find my fruity flower wine amongst the very best
My leaves they can detoxify and there are antioxidants there
And so many other health benefits that they boldly bear

I am a simple subject of so many myths and games
Perhaps that's why people have give me so many names
I retain my glamours green when all your lawns are yellow
So respect me and regard me as a really remarkable fellow

Awakening from my daydream and as I homeward turned
I mulled over those magic moments and all that I had learned
In life, as in this short story, never judge a novel by its cover
There may be powers and promises within to learn and to discover

Alpine Meadow Magic

On a morning ramble in the cold, crisp mountain air
Gazing in awe at the beauty of all God's grandeur there
I climb over the crest of a stone-strewn rocky bluff
The climb was strenuous, really rugged and rough

When what to my wandering eye did suddenly appear
But a wild and wonderous sight, so precious, so dear
A magic mountain meadow with masses of alpine flowers
A cornucopia of colours that overwhelms and overpowers

Words can't quite capture this splendid and striking scene
The sheer size and beauty of a unique spectacle so serene
Sensational and more stunning in each and every way
Than the finest picture ever painted by a Renoir or Monet

Wild and free in this whimsical wilderness world apart
It frees the mind and stirs a warmth in any weary heart
Paintbrushes bowing briefly in a slight sierra breeze
It's so relaxing and puts a tired and troubled soul at ease

Heathers and lupines and even an occasional mountain Lilly
Saxifrages, monkey flowers and some vallerians so frilly
Purples and blues, pinks, whites and even yellows
With the greenest of greens makes me feel so mellow

Whistling mountain marmots a grazing mountain goat
A gentle grizzly on a distant hill or a small but skittery stoat
So many mammals and birds, like soaring eagles too
Whiskey jacks, grouse and ptarmigans, to name but a few

Mountain spires that seem to split stunning azure skies
Glaciers and snow-covered peaks a feast for tired eyes
Shimmering streams cascading down from waterfalls on high
And gentle winds that sing to me in a soft and gentle sigh

Those memories still cling to me and play on in my mind
A magical mountain masterpiece so heavenly divined
We were gladly gifted the bountiful beauty of the great outdoors
So please protect and preserve it for everyone - mine and yours

Summer Sunset

There is magic in the heavens just at eventide
When the sun, in a rosy glow, begins to slowly slide
It touches the horizon where the sea meets the land
And paints nature canvas with an adept artist's hand

Hues and blended colours coalesce in the sea and sky
Tinting the clouds and waves together as they pass slowly by
Where earth ends and sky begins, the eye can scarcely tell
As a captivated mind is enraptured by this inspiring spell

As the kaleidoscope of colours fade the winds begin to die
And the sweet Nightingale's song drifts down slowly from high
A pensive note of peace envelops the landscape all around
The melodious melody enchants with tranquility unbound

The bubbling brook adds its voice to the departing light of day
As shadows creep across the sea and descend upon the bay
Trees along the shoreline cast sinewy silhouettes on the sand
Like the long fingers playing piano on a concert pianist's hand

Gently the colours fade as daylight slowly spirals towards night
And a certain sadness comes with the expiring glory of the light
As an unseen hand draws the curtain on the soon-departing day
And the golden gate of the sunset all too soon passes away

This is only a picture for no poet could describe
The wondrous beauty of a stunning sunset just at eventide
So ask yourself this question at the closing of the day
While you recall with reverence at what just passed away

Why can't this paradigm of peace be shared by everyone
And spread across the lands until all conflicts are undone
Surely sunsets are messengers, a harbinger of what should be
Telling us to live together in a calm and placid harmony

About the Author

James Glassford is a retired physician who has been blessed with the opportunity to live in one of the most beautiful and awe-inspiring places on earth - Vancouver Island. Nature's remarkable gifts begin at his doorstep and in the seashore of the Salish Seas, as seen from his deck. Throughout his life, whether it be in the far north, the rocky mountains or here on Vancouver Island, he has admired and been in awe of the natural world. He has spent countless hours hiking, admiring and observing Nature. It is a soothing balm to the soul and a respite from the challenges and frustrations of daily living. His credo can be summed up in the words that Lord Byron wrote:

"There is a pleasure in the pathless woods

There is a rapture on the lonely shore

There is a society where none intrudes

By the deep sea and music in its roar

I love not man the less but Nature more"